BLAST OFF!

ALL ABOUT
SPACE SHUTTLES

Miriam Gross

PowerKiDS
press™

New York

Published in 2009 by The Rosen Publishing Group, Inc.
29 East 21st Street, New York, NY 10010

First Edition

Editor: Joanne Randolph
Book Design: Greg Tucker
Photo Researcher: Jessica Gerweck

Photo Credits: Cover, pp. 5, 11,15, 17, 19 © Getty Images; pp. 7, 13, 21 © AFP/Getty Images; p. 9 Shutterstock.com.

Library of Congress Cataloging-in-Publication Data

Gross, Miriam J.
   All about space shuttles / Miriam Gross. — 1st ed.
        p. cm. — (Blast off!)
   Includes bibliographical references and index.
   ISBN 978-1-4358-2738-7 (library binding) — ISBN 978-1-4358-3136-0 (pbk.)
ISBN 978-1-4358-3142-1 (6-pack)
   1. Space shuttles—Juvenile literature. I. Title.
   TL795.515.G76 2009
   629.44'1—dc22
                                            2008030437

Manufactured in the United States of America

CONTENTS

SPACE PLANE   4

HISTORY OF SPACE SHUTTLES   6

PARTS OF A SPACE SHUTTLE   8

BLASTING OFF INTO SPACE   10

RETURNING TO EARTH   12

USES FOR THE SPACE SHUTTLE   14

THE SPACE SHUTTLE *COLUMBIA*   16

THE SPACE SHUTTLE *CHALLENGER*   18

THE SPACE SHUTTLE *DISCOVERY*   20

WHAT IS NEXT?   22

GLOSSARY   23

INDEX   24

WEB SITES   24

Look up in the sky! Is that a bird? Is that a plane? No, it is the space shuttle! Space shuttles roar into space like rockets and fly back down to Earth like airplanes. When they get to space, space shuttles orbit Earth, or fly around it in a circle. They can stay in space for weeks at a time. The same shuttle can fly to space and back to Earth many times.

People call the space shuttle a workhorse because it does so many jobs in space. Space shuttles make it easier for **astronauts** to explore, or visit and learn more about, space.

Here the space shuttle *Discovery* takes off from Cape Canaveral, Florida. The
shuttle was carrying a part for the International Space Station, which is a satellite

A government organization called the National Aeronautics and Space Administration (NASA) began sending people into space on rockets in 1961. Launching, or pushing off, into space destroyed these early rockets. Each rocket could be used only once.

NASA wanted to send people into space more often, but it cost too much money and was wasteful. In 1972, NASA began working on a new kind of spacecraft that could be reused. The first space shuttle ever built was called *Enterprise*. It was built in 1977 but was used only for testing.

People are shown here visiting the *Enterprise* at the Smithsonian's Steven F. Udvar-Hazy Center, in Virginia. The *Enterprise* was flown in 16 test flights.

There are three main parts of a space shuttle. They are the orbiter, the rocket boosters, and the external, or outside, **fuel** tank. The rocket boosters push the space shuttle off from the ground. The external fuel tank holds the gases that the shuttle burns. It is the only part of the space shuttle that cannot be reused.

The orbiter is where the astronauts stay. It has places for them to sleep and cook and large windows so they can look out into space. The orbiter also carries the cargo, or the objects that the astronauts carry into space.

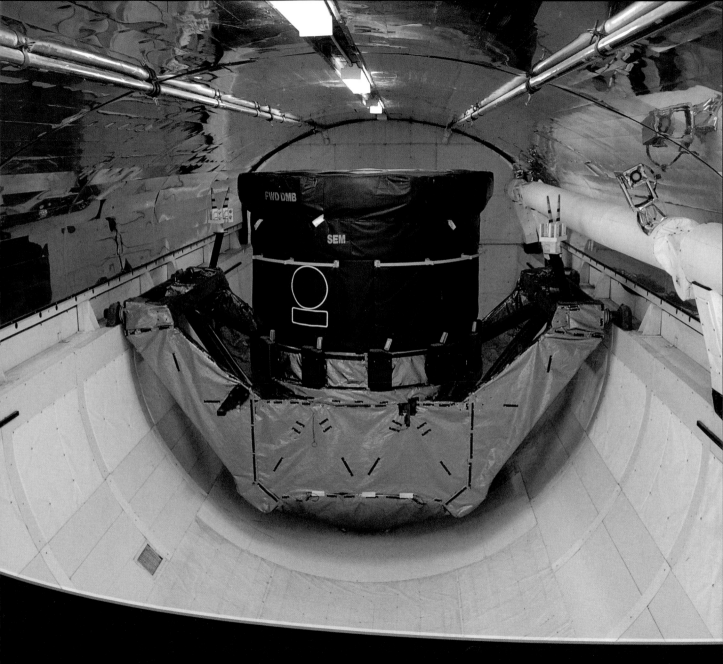

This photo shows the cargo bay inside a space shuttle orbiter. The cargo bay is about the size of a school bus and can carry up to 50,000 pounds (22,680 kg).

A shuttle weighs 4.5 million pounds (2 million kg) when it is ready to launch. Rocket boosters push the heavy shuttle off the ground with great force.

Two minutes after the shuttle has taken off, the rocket boosters drop off from the orbiter and land in the ocean. Ships find them and take them back to land to use again. After nine minutes, the external fuel tank also drops off. It burns up on its way back to Earth. **Engines** on the orbiter then fire to put the shuttle on the right path to orbit Earth.

The part that is shooting out fire here is one of the rocket boosters. Heat and gas combine to create a huge amount of force, which lets the shuttle blast into space.

When the shuttle is ready to come back to Earth, it slows down. It starts flying lower, or closer to Earth, in its orbit. When the shuttle reaches Earth's **atmosphere**, it flies with its wings, like an airplane.

As the orbiter comes closer to the ground, wheels pop out from the bottom. The orbiter reaches the runway, and it rolls down the runway as a plane does. It goes very fast, so a **parachute** opens from the back to help slow it down. Soon the orbiter comes safely to a stop.

Here is a space shuttle with its parachute open. The runway for the shuttle is 15,000 feet (4,572 m) long and 300 feet (91 m) wide, with 1,000 feet (305 m) extra on each end for safety.

A space shuttle can do many jobs. Space shuttles carry astronauts to and from **space stations**, such as *Mir* and the International Space Station. They can help carry up supplies and parts to build the space stations.

Space shuttles can be used to launch **satellites** into orbit. They can also bring astronauts out to fix satellites that have broken in space.

Space shuttles can also carry special labs where astronauts can run **experiments**. In the labs, they can test how things work in space, where there is no **gravity**.

The space shuttle *Discovery* is shown here as it gets ready to dock with the ISS. *Discovery* was bringing a piece to add to the space station.

The first space shuttle to fly into space was called *Columbia*. It first took off in 1981. On its first flight, it stayed in orbit for over two days. *Columbia* stayed in service for over 20 years.

On February 1, 2003, *Columbia* was on its way back to Earth after a **mission** when something went wrong. The shuttle broke apart in the sky before it could land. All seven astronauts on board died.

It was a terrible **tragedy**. NASA stopped shuttle flights for a while. They wanted to make space shuttles safer before launching them again.

Here *Columbia* rides on the back of a special 747 airplane, which carries the space shuttle when it is not being used. *Columbia* flew 23 missions before it broke apart in 2003.

Challenger was the second space shuttle launched into orbit. It made its first flight in 1983.

On January 28, 1986, *Challenger* lifted off for its tenth mission. Among the astronauts on board was a teacher named Christa McAuliffe.

Just after take-off, the *Challenger* blew up in the air. All seven astronauts died in this **accident**. Many people had watched the launch on TV. The whole country felt very sad about the astronauts. NASA did not fly any more space shuttles for the next two years.

This is the crew of the 1986 *Challenger* flight, who were lost just 73 seconds after launch. Christa McAuliffe is the second person from the left in the back row.

Discovery was built to be safer than *Challenger*. It made its first flight in 1988. After the *Columbia* tragedy in 2003, *Discovery* was made even safer. The *Discovery* was ready to return to space in July 2005.

Discovery has now launched into space more than 25 times. It has flown important missions. It brought many astronauts and gear into space to build the International Space Station. *Discovery* has also launched unmanned spacecraft to Venus, Jupiter, and the Sun.

Here *Discovery* sits on the launchpad getting ready to blast off in May 2008. The shuttle carried a part of the ISS, called Kibo, into space.

Space shuttles have flown more than 120 missions. They have helped us explore space more than we ever could before.

NASA will **retire** the space shuttles when it has finished building the International Space Station. A new kind of spacecraft will take the space shuttle's place. It will also bring people into space, but it will travel even farther. By 2020, NASA hopes to send people back to the Moon. After that, they hope to send people to Mars and maybe even to other planets.

GLOSSARY

ACCIDENT (AK-sih-dent) An unexpected and sometimes bad thing that happens.

ASTRONAUTS (AS-truh-nots) People who are trained to travel in outer space.

ATMOSPHERE (AT-muh-sfeer) The gases around an object in space. On Earth, this is air.

ENGINES (EN-jinz) Machines that use fuel to move an object.

EXPERIMENTS (ik-SPER-uh-ments) Sets of actions or steps taken to learn more about something.

FUEL (FYOOL) Something used to make warmth or power.

GRAVITY (GRA-vih-tee) The natural force that causes objects to move toward the center of Earth.

MISSION (MIH-shun) A special job.

PARACHUTE (PAR-uh-shoot) A large piece of cloth shaped like an umbrella that is used to slow down a falling or moving object.

RETIRE (rih-TY-ur) To decide not to use anymore.

SATELLITES (SA-tih-lyts) Natural or manmade objects that circle a planet in space.

SPACE STATIONS (SPAYS STAY-shunz) Large satellites where humans can work and live for long periods of time in space and that can also be a base for sending other spacecraft farther into space.

TRAGEDY (TRA-jeh-dee) A very sad event.

INDEX

A
astronauts, 4, 8, 14, 16, 18, 20
atmosphere, 12

E
Earth, 4, 10, 12, 16
engines, 10
experiments, 14

G
gravity, 14

M
mission(s), 16, 18, 20, 22

N
National Aeronautics and Space Administration (NASA), 6, 16, 18, 22

O
orbiter, 8, 10, 12

P
parachute, 12
people, 4, 6, 22

R
rocket(s), 4, 6

S
satellites, 14
sky, 4, 16
space, 4, 6, 8, 14, 16, 20, 22
space station(s), 14, 20, 22

T
tragedy, 16, 20

W
workhorse, 4

WEB SITES

Due to the changing nature of Internet links, PowerKids Press has developed an online list of Web sites related to the subject of this book. This site is updated regularly. Please use this link to access the list:
www.powerkidslinks.com/blastoff/shuttles/